Why Do eaves Change Color?

A **Just Ask** Book

Hi, my name is Christopher!

by Chris Arvetis
and Carole Palmer

illustrated by James Buckley

Copyright © 1986 by Rand McNally & Company
All rights reserved
Printed in Italy
Library of Congress Catalog Card Number: 85-63020

CHILDRENS PRESS CHOICE

A Rand McNally title selected for educational distribution
ISBN 0-516-09811-X

1986 SCHOOL AND LIBRARY EDITION

Look at the leaves.
Something has happened.
The leaves aren't green
any more.
They are changing color.

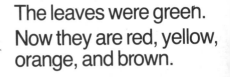

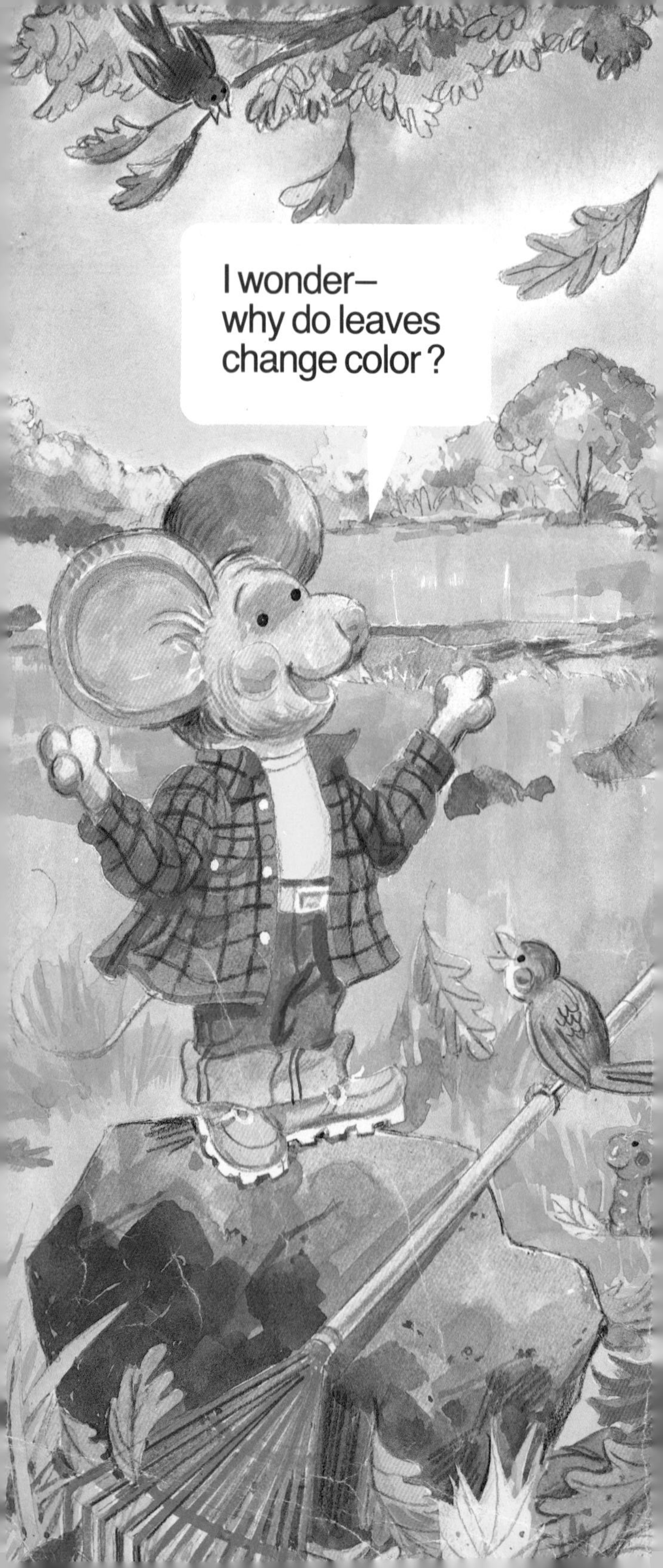
I wonder–
why do leaves
change color?

Well, I don't know.
But I'll bet someone does.
Our friend the squirrel
lives in a tree.
He must know something
about leaves.
Let's ask him.

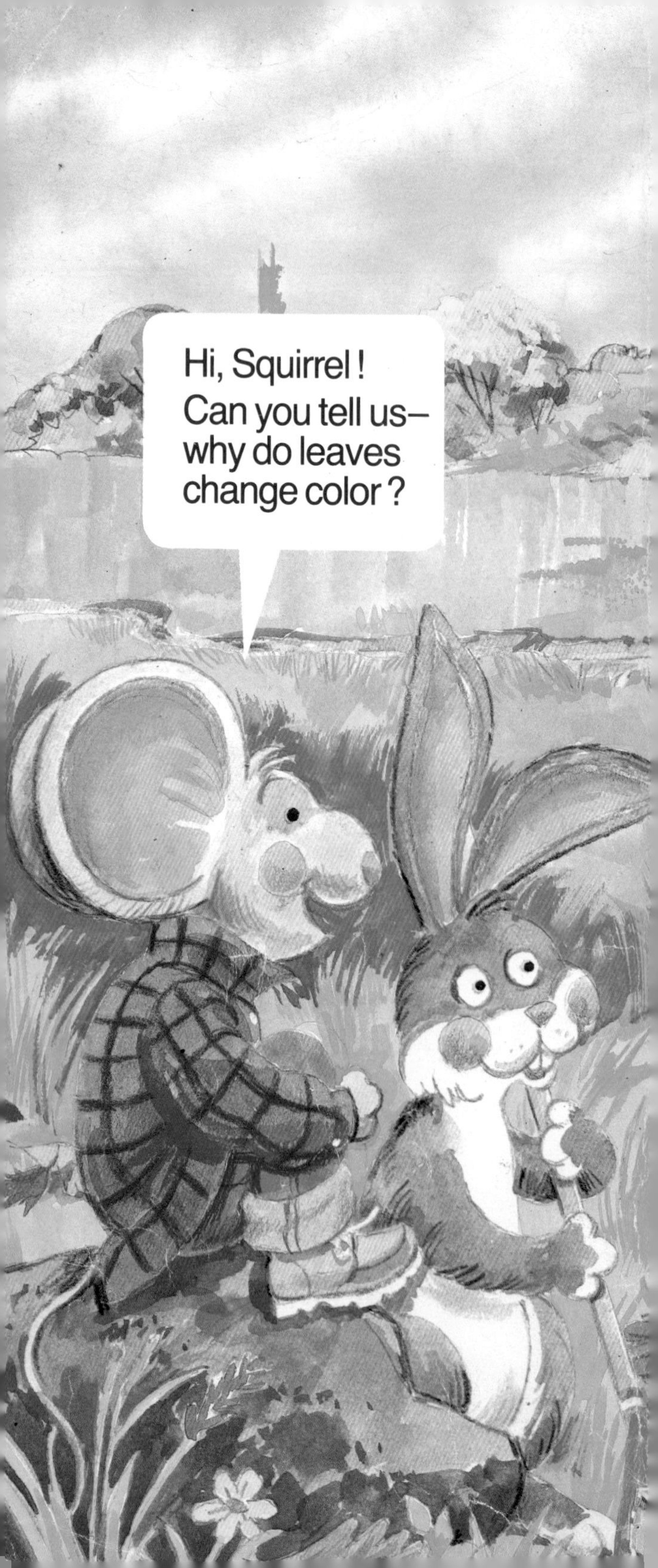
Hi, Squirrel! Can you tell us– why do leaves change color?

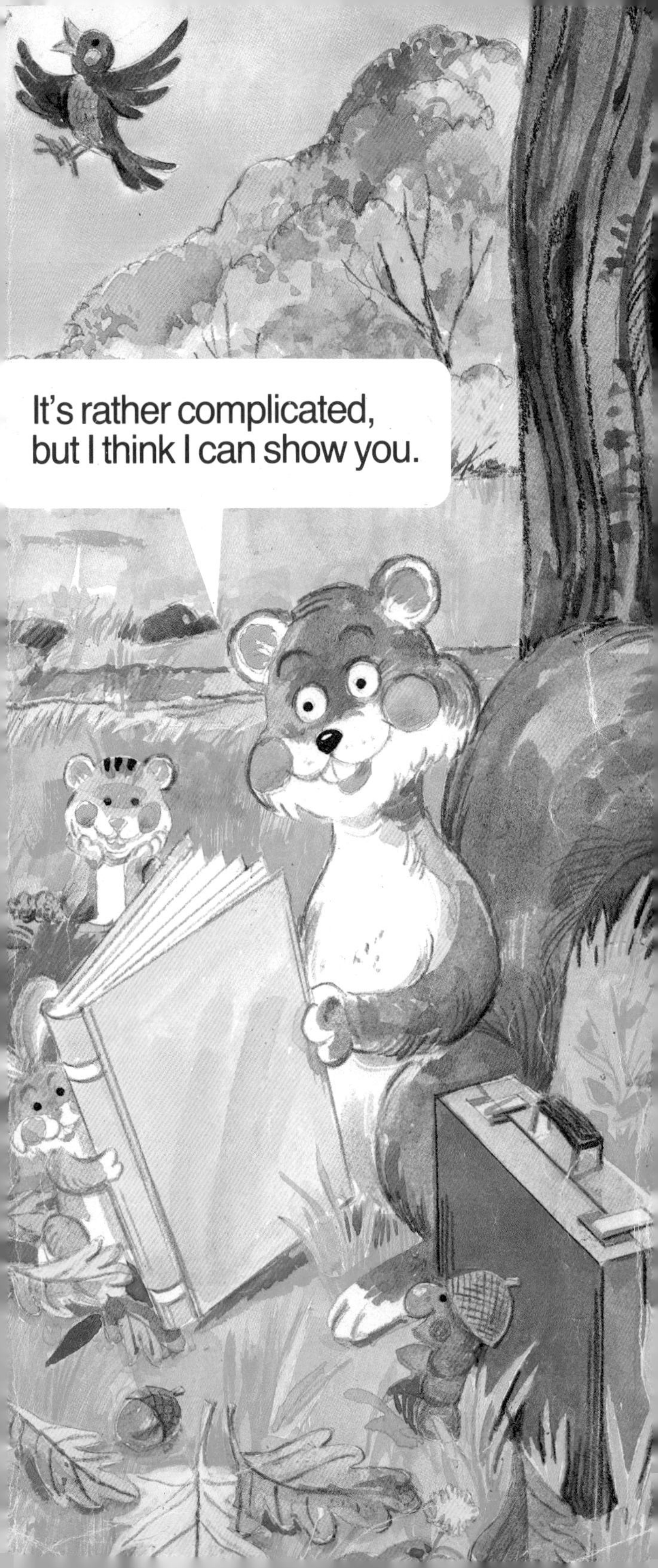
It's rather complicated, but I think I can show you.

Try to think back
to springtime.
That's when the little
buds appear on the
branches of the trees.
Each little bud is the
beginning of a new leaf.

The sun warms the bud and the new leaf begins to grow. As the leaf grows, it starts to make its own food.

Each leaf is like a tiny food factory.

The leaf uses sunlight, things in the air, water, and a green matter called CHLOROPHYLL.

Say CHLOROPHYLL with me.

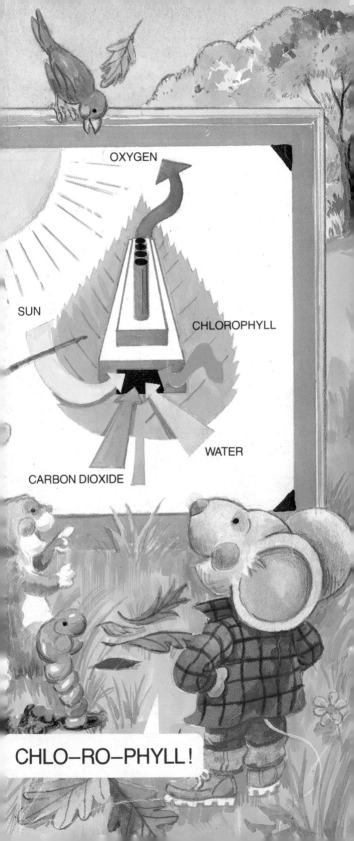

As the leaf makes food, the chlorophyll keeps the leaf green and healthy.

The leaf also has other colors in it, but the green chlorophyll covers them up.

Let me show you.

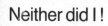

I'll color this yellow.
Then I'll color over
it with green.
See!
The green covers
up the yellow.

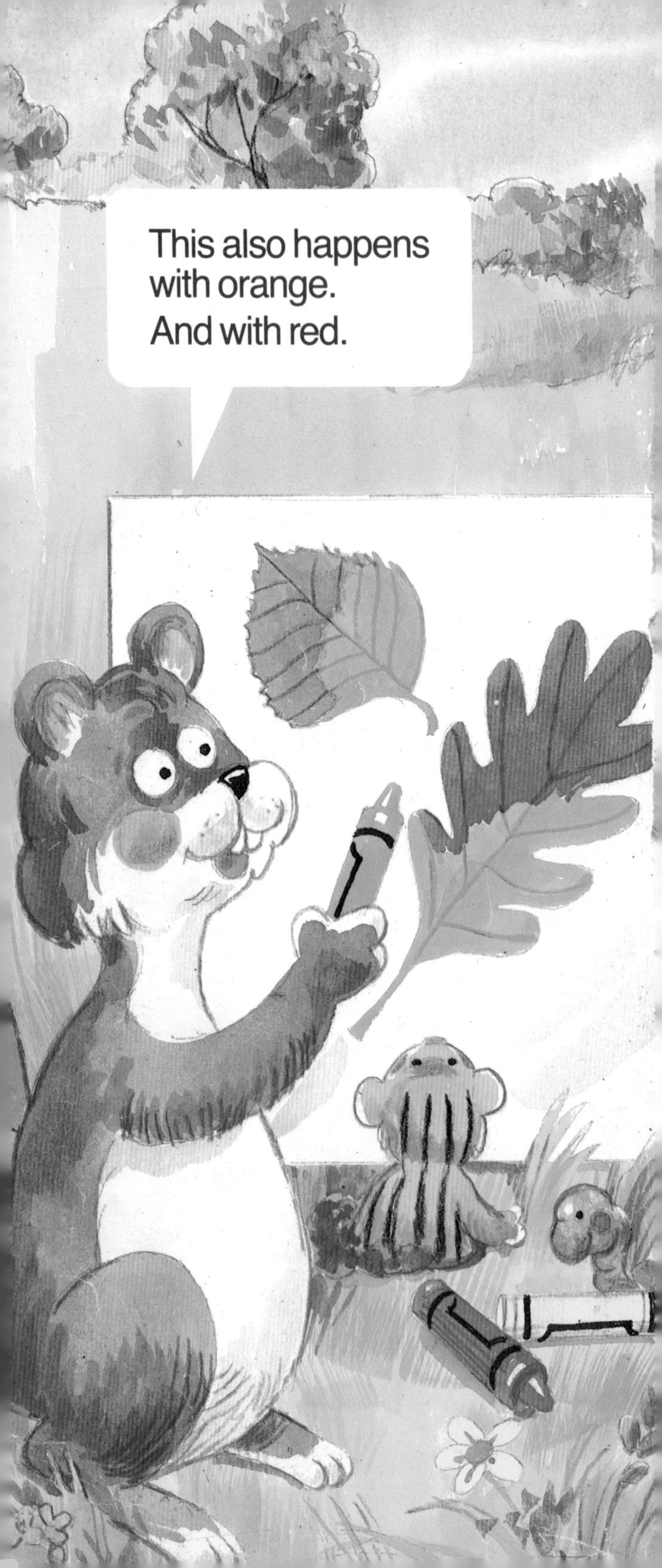
This also happens with orange.
And with red.

And even with light brown. In the leaf, the green chlorophyll covers up the other colors so we see only green leaves.

When the fall season begins, the leaf starts to die.

There is less sunlight because the days are shorter.

The leaf no longer makes food.

The green chlorophyll breaks up and disappears.

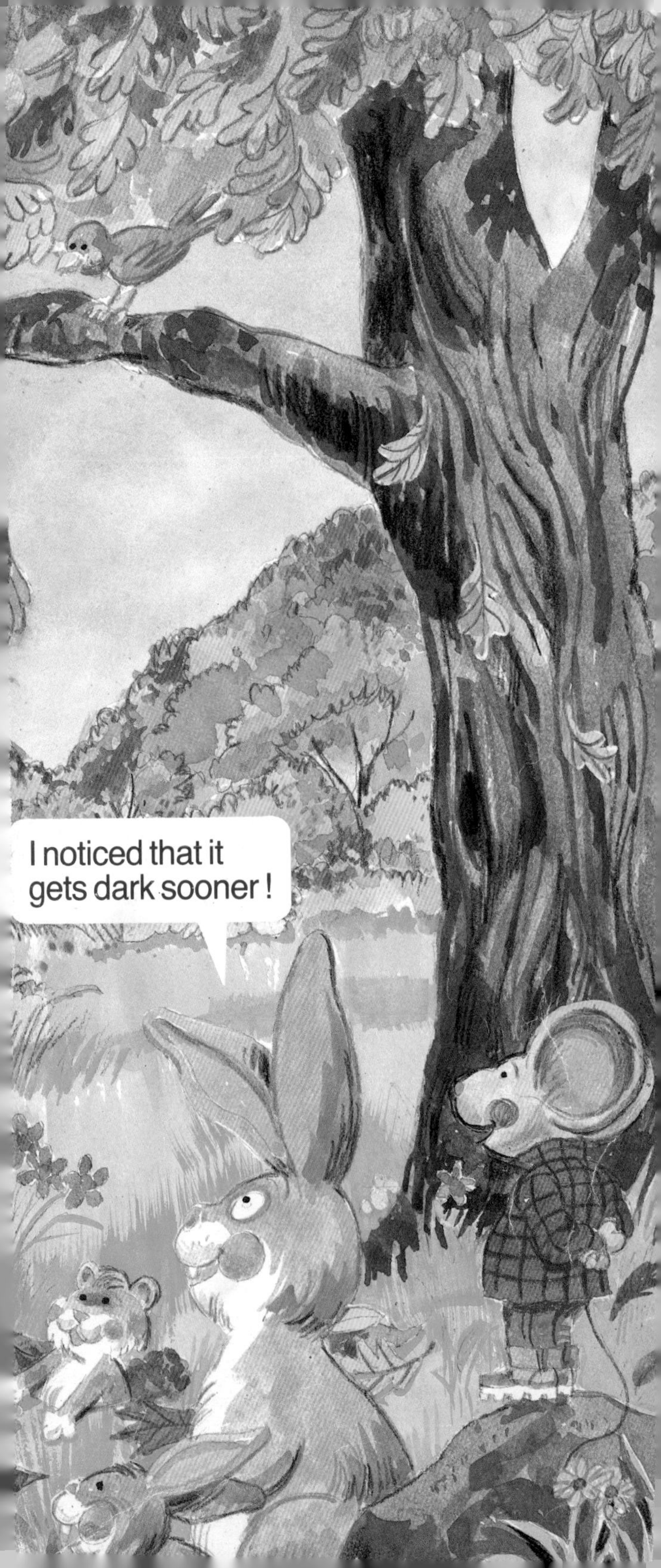
I noticed that it
gets dark sooner !

As the chlorophyll disappears, the other colors show through.

The leaf begins to change color.

Now the leaf is yellow or orange or red or brown or a mixture of these colors.

get it !

Look at the leaves falling
all around us.

See the yellow ones, the
orange ones, and all
of the colors.

Now do you think you know—
why leaves change color?

When the leaf begins to die, the leaf no longer makes food.

The chlorophyll breaks down and the green color begins to disappear.

All the hidden colors— the reds, yellows, oranges, and browns— can be seen.

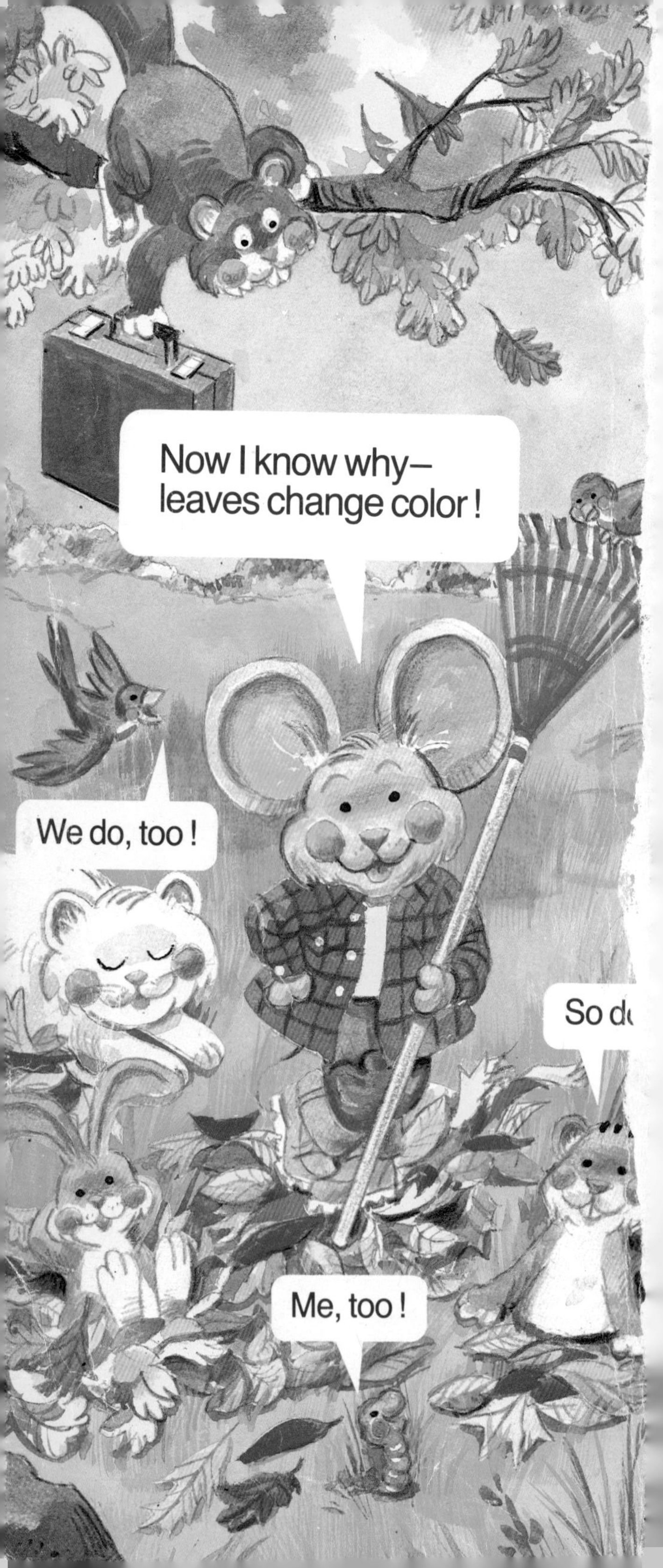
Now I know why–
leaves change color!
We do, too!
So d
Me, too!